NOTIONS OF A MIRROR

ANTHONY HOWELL

NOTIONS OF A MIRROR

Poems previously uncollected
1964-1982

for Sue
with best wishes
Anthony

Anvil Press Poetry

Published in 1983
by Anvil Press Poetry Ltd
69 King George Street London SE10 8PX
ISBN 0 85646 104 0

Typeset and printed in England
at the Arc & Throstle Press
Todmorden Lancs

This book is published
with financial assistance from
The Arts Council of Great Britain

Contents:

   *   *   *   *   *   *   *   *   *   *

TICKLISHNESS

The bird she cannot bear
Walks with tiny strides
Attacking here a grain.
Her belly shrinks before
Suggested promenades
Of its feathery idea.

But such a tease as this
No ocean dare resist
Or lunatic ignore.
Imagine either fate:
An overbalanced wave,
Asphyxiating mirth.

Surrender is a fort.
The cornered ball uncurls
Inviting beak to nest.
This confuses predator
With timid prey impaled
Upon a broken sword.

ANIMAL LOVER

1 Without Titles

(i)
Crepuscular.
Her rationale the non-competitive cheetah's.
(Intellect of absolutely no importance
Except as it affects certain external flexions.)

The mouth, shaping for its own benefit
A variety of syllables.

(ii)
Hot-blooded diet, parded love
That could never adapt to prosaic situations
(Pavements file down the claws)
Nor survive the tritest of breakfasts.

2 Towards Night the Jungle Laps the Waterhole

Aubades haunt the aviary.
Those who are accustomed to devouring darkness
Slide into each other for repose.

(The well fed, meticulous hubbub
Of the herd — snufflers at the trough
Indulge in trunky intercourse.)

Hatred in epitome, or is it love:
The way those big cats mock
The meat of their keeper?

3   Six Legged Odalisque with Wings

(i)
Freedom: a regressive sense
That manacles her to herself;
Haggard blood paces out a constitutional
Against the ribcage.

This is the innermost, arcane
Gymnopedia. Butterflies
In the tummy cause her to rest
A hand on the escorting wrist.

Touch and the wings fold.

(ii)
When the tigress dare not venture
Without a mask to lull censure,
When those insipids, the butterflies
Make up their much wider eyes,

Flirt we then in the moon's mirror,
The bed, the retentive pool,
The killing bottle: facets blur

All living stones, my pet, and clever
Boys with gauze to catch you in
Shall fix the pin;
Spread your wings to dry forever.

4   The Decalogue Forbids Idolatry

Nothing cleans the key to an inadmissible
Room, and it is only a fool
Such as Francis talks to animals;
Thus she preserves the vault's quiet

(Her breath waking no echo) as
The vault preserves us, all the more

Abandoned in her sleep — a beautiful gibbon.
Turned from the peaceable kingdom,
The wolf would have her stroke his whisker,
Howls for a glance, if not the look

That changed his mate to salt.
Let me insist, there are no true idols.

DROUGHT

According to the eye in the leaf
the lawn frays at the hem to a smoky horizon.
(This is from the height of two feet.)

Lean, telescoping stalks survey the enemy sky,
trepidatious are the ranks waiting in their
bladed trenches. Gradually the afternoons brown.

The grasses have a hard time, summer:
the fragile curl up & die lighter
at the ankles of their companions, the leaner

suck the marrows of the dead. To the eye
in the leaf, the robin's, savage constant
of any scale or dimension, flurries

of holocaust are apparent but too largely
out of focus: how the grasses pull together
as best they can, how few stagger to their feet.

But the robin cocks himself for the next
significant intelligence in his own battle,
several feet subterranean in this weather

which affects us all. The eye & to all intents
the foliage on which he pends, on
which to some extent his prey depends,

disregard each others' tribulations.
While strident in seven-league, accident-prone
boots, in their party frocks and formal

decorations, go the heavy gods who actuate
these wars, these eye-sores on the lawn,
bickering & informing against their relations.

DEFICIENCIES OF TOURISM
—*after Southerne*

Language proved intransitive currency:
Ruined, for all his ready cash,
This shady protector donned protective shades.
Blind in the glare of what was apparent
His was a dim view of the sights:
A sultry beach that brandished scorching thighs,
A casino, an appealing promenade.
—Edifice designed for temporary strollers,
Tourists and unbelievers, those
For whom all pleasure is the tense approach.
(They stalk their prey, they stumble
On a carcass. Habit dulls disgust;
While the decay that inspires the air
Cankers their taste-buds.) Would contempt
Familiarise him with incurable foods?

Why blame exotic brochures? His visits there
Had advertised her privacy.
He had installed the alien chefs
Attendant on her scented meats:
Savour of hygiene, frigid the worms and germs.
Nightmares mauled each hushed locality,
Not an apology salved the bruise;
He deemed appropriate compensation this gilt-edged
Complaint: he specified a resort!
Never had he bargained for a neighbourhood
—Whose interior the most strenuous of excursions
Fails to penetrate; whose revelations
Barely appear when eyes grow accustomed,
Lips inexpectant, as if blind:
A continent, whose laughter drums repeat.

Inarticulate meat, the camouflage
Of the passive voiced, the flesh-made-word:
A lonely waitress loosens her apron,
Examines her hidden smile,
Serves herself black beer beneath plain trees.

BURGLARY BETWEEN MEALS

And when it ceased, the fridge's buzz
Which seemed, while his eyes were out of action,
Crickets, caged, in a porcelain house
Where peacock and pagoda tinted
Water-coloured pools, it was
The hush of startled legs, alarum's
Absence woke him to the scream
Whose echo tinkled china and despaired.

Roused from the dream which had kept him snug
As pekinese in matron's lap,
He yawned, and stretched his neck erect.
The thermostat which caused the shock
Preserved an optimistic chill
About his lunch. But fridges dream,
Jolting their once haunted goods.
He rubbed his eyes to accept the apparent.

Once unveiled, what feast emerged
Bright as his first view of Saint Mark's?
Did fruits display exotic rinds
With which to advertise their favours?
Yes — but horror quelled the joy
Foretasted in what first had seemed
An edible bouquet: arrangement
Dedicated to being munched.

Prior to his nap, a fridge had stood
Loaded with fish, perhaps, or fowl,
Or marquetry inlaid in aspic,
Celery, Corinthian columns
Comestible, a jug of ale—
But this had changed, though vacuum-sealed
The door, when opened wide, revealed
A bric-à-brac of things portrayed.

There in a cabinet brittle deer
Froze upon shelves: menagerie
Of speechless birds, unsnorting horses.
Executed, baked in clay,
While the graceful strokes of a master's brush
With tactful touches stilled the life.
It made him yearn for Persia where
The lions rage in living rock.

Thus hungered Midas, peel and knife
Become one solid ornament,
Who wanted subtler riches than
A brazen lady's Jovial fall
In showers of coin, and wondered what.
Wiser Solomon, who begged
An attribute, a ray of light:
One slender fork to prick his meat.

That wizard never wasted time.
Djinns might obey a butterfly's tantrum,
Vanishing palaces with their wings.
Therefore he did bask in Sheba,
Feed upon a fattening land.
The modern is the daintier man:
A conjurer, self-hypnotised,
Bewitching what should be consumed.

So Grace addresses tedious thanks
Till breasts metamorphose into gourds:
And blooms congealing in a vase
Only fail to terrorise
The speculative nose because
Curators of a food museum
Take great care to restrain the exhibits
Under frames of proper glass.

What some receive should not be sought:
Ability to turn the clouds
To flowers drinking in a glass
—No more to wilt, but wind-bereaved,
The canvas dead. For he who sat
In his china shop felt like a cat,
Fastidious about the paws,
But sniffed a bull's ingathered sneeze.

NOTIONS OF A MIRROR

1

Yes, you can take that away,
But leave the similar objects as they are
—Visibly, they fill themselves.

It all exactly fits:
Here, and there
A mass of shapely things.

And those, in a trance of manifestation
Rocketing from their place,
What are they called?

2

Each deep face
Echoes our own feelings
—Rather than drink you in

An urge to whisper nothings:
"Call me a Wishful, nevertheless
We might be little

Better than relations,
Even the blinds display a space as querulous,
There is no room for more."

EXAMINING MINE, IMAGINING YOURS

Hand on the left will make no sign
Of movement unless sure
The route affords strategic pockets
Vital to retreat: it treads
With a sloth's anxiety,
Fixed in a bright globe of quiet.

Right hand relies on tactics:
Crouches to consider,
Jumps! Brutally severe, he curls
And spreads his nails, attesting claws
That basked within a carcass.
Wrist he may mistake for throat.

That hand's unblinking charmers,
Stroking the callous palm
Just as one should the belly of a cat;
This hand's jungle, vase of flowers,
Nesting the sloth in fingers
Curious as a team of naturalists;

Scornful of strait-jacket gloves;
Not animated puppets but
Supporters of unstable gods:
Firm as ancient clouds, your hands
Hover on their jointed stems
Like thoughts difficult to arrange.

EXTRANEOUS FIXTURES

Tenements where everything is repaired
Except the tenants. What are they
But weights for the resident furniture
To be sat on by? Nor may they strain
The divan plump with maladies,
For what they wear they do not own.
Dish-washers hardly deal with dishes.

Each house helps another up the hill:
No tenant asks for like support
From neighbours when to slip outside
And rap the nearest door allows
Absence to enter theirs and change
The lock and key to all that's loaned—
More phantom then, being exorcised.

How flat the stare, daring no smash
Though trains trail goods in bulk across
Embankment windows and the sun
Sit in each park to keep it warm:
These tenants waste such hours indoors
Mere body heat they fade from chairs,
And poplars shake like displaced souls.

MYTH AMONG BOULDERS

I

Much less vainly might you peel
A dragon scale by scale by scale
      Than fathom how Medusa fixed the hero.

II

As she feels your forceps pinch
            This labyrinth heaves tentacles
Enthralling those who fail to blink.

III

Then and there the punctual cock
Crows derisive doodledoos.
      Shadow steps into your shoes.

FEMINA DESERTA

The Maker takes his one siesta
In this idle country bare
Of milk and honey, mud and straw:

A garden where the presence of
Proprietor diminishes
The space elsewhere embedding things.

Does meditation magnify
A moment or elaborate
Events to dress the poverty?

The mind's a spider in this heat:
Metaphor's geometry
Must extend a lengthy net,

Whose rigging may intend towards
A hillock where a certain bush
Is said to quench the thirst with fire—

But nomads in retirement stare
Beyond the littered littoral
Where shepherds reprimand their sheep:

They tell of cairns reviewing cairns
Already seen, and further still
A riddle waving eager tail:

Underneath whose haunches fur
Explains the smell that captivates
Aroma conscious bedouin:

Holding a breath for ever and ever,
Saturating lungs
Jealous of what each inhales.

Pernicious breeze in nostrils able
To divine a lost oasis
By the reek of its mirage.

Here Solitude herself remains
Inert — for all the splash of pails
In the well available.

Guess ahead, suppose a city
Helmeted with mosque,
Flinging the lance of its minaret.

But will a hand succeed in crossing
Such a virginal expanse
While struggling against repose?

Perhaps the never pictured mosque
Which rinses clean all vision stained
By naked light cannot appear?

The further place forbids a visit:
Dwellers there may be supposed
To own no word for boundary;

Where afternoons direct migrations,
And each profile of tall bone
Gives away an obvious name,

And if and when a finger twitches
Surfaces of satin stir
In hieroglyphic labyrinths.

But as we near the stranger stars
Our singers cease to innovate,
They pause at more familiar nouns.

A savage blaze upon the forehead
Of a brigand's horse describes
That ambush which the sun prepares:

Before whose rampant haze the date road
Falters. Our approach explodes
The landmarks — into old dry birds.

The desert thinks the vultures limping
Over her reflection are
The pockmarks of her dry oases.

Horror in the gleam of joy
That blinds the fly who crawls among
Her lips towards a laser tongue!

At arm's length is the sun whose grin
Certifies he values her
Above his other predators.

She turns away, inviting night's
Brown eyelids down to soothe the shells
Azure as mosques, her nested eyes.

Hip to hip she lies with night
Though envious of the splendid gouts
Replenishing his open mouth;

Her own reserve is curdled somewhere
Silent — and for this her nerves
Must go to vague extremities.

That she may blossom at the tight
Antipodes of every root
Sky becomes a tree of rain:

A thunder tree who clenches cloud,
The torso of a liquid god
Which branches out in muscled flood,

And shakes the fledglings from her shells
Till tunes revolve like little pins
Arranged around a cylinder.

The desert stretches forth her neck
And shifts her weight — a sluggish ocean
Pleased the rudder alters her.

Then cacti germinate and fix
Their set of brooches there before
The miracle evaporates

In sand whose tautly hollow sound
Is evidence, although an ear
Will never prove the reservoir.

Such secrecy envenoms flesh
And suckles what prefers to wriggle
Like a vein, immersed in dust.

No faithful dove invades these waves
To whisper the obscenities
Of any charming rainbow demon.

Flash! The thunder came and went.
That momentary deluge seemed
A phantom of annunciation.

Mockeries of vegetation
Are engendered thus, to jilt
Her thirstiness and leave her frozen.

Leave her freezing in the sun
Whose cymbals deafen when they clash,
While fever beats its rapid drum:

Fever which insists mosquitoes
Darn upon her famished realm
A needle-pointed zodiac:

Because without one stitch of green
Embroidery, spread-eagled, bound
By thongs which tighten while they dry.

A kind of shame, the drought chastises
Wilderness, that naked ground
Where revelations feel their way.

LOSS OF A LANGUAGE

Before it shut, your mouth
Uttered the last word.
Darkness covered your face,
The distressed waters
Writhed like incensed adders.

Overstrung, the crack
Of each high tension wire
Blackened night:
Our bridges bucked,
Many a road ran wild.

How did who return?
Wading the knee-deep lakes
To touch familiar walls
Strange with green, while roads
Waited in immense reels.

Sewage foams at the tap.
Furniture and sheep
Glide beyond our reach
Beneath the empty bridges
Polished of graffiti.

Left with an aftertaste
Of unremembered names
Bitter as salt for sugar.
Dong, bong, dong.
The tongue lurches in a tower.

MODERN SONNETS

1

Wonder appears when union occurs.
Union occurs where conflict appears
To be. Conflict appears when conflict
Appears to be union. Conflict occurs
Where union appears to be wonder
When any. Union appears when wonder
Appears to be union where any conflict.

Wonder occurs where union appears
To be conflict when any conflict occurs.
Union appears when conflict appears
To be conflict where any union appears
To be. Conflict occurs where conflict
Appears to be union when any wonder
Appears to be union. Conflict appears.

2

The nearer the sense you are here
The further you turn yourself from me
The nearer the sense you are there
The further the sense I am here.

The further the sense you are here
The nearer you turn yourself to me
The further the sense you are there
The nearer the sense I am there.

The nearer you turn you to yourself
The further I turn myself from you
The nearer the sense I am here.

The nearer I turn myself to you
The further the sense I am there
I turn the further me to myself.

DREAMT LIVES

And always saying no to say everything,
Never nodding to affirm, and to deny everything,
Forever not at home, not to say anything,
Hardly conversational, and to affirm anything
In narrow clean mansions forever not at home.

You decayed in an untidy house
Fattening on the highways among friends
Who grew up in rambling stables: and to affirm anything
A market place with unknown rooms,
Accessible departments and outdoors.

Who grew up admitting less?
—Refusing every bit in rambling stables,
And among hermits who died in private alcoves
Among lovers and deserted squares
With known rooms and never saying no.

I was to begin my life, you decayed
In constrained circumstances and outdoors:
Dwindling in alleys among enemies
Taciturn about the lot in small neat houses
—To say just that among the angels.

I flourished in a neat house,
Accepting all that came saying nothing,
Voluble about the lot, and affirming nothing,
And never saying no, silent about little,
Shaking head seldom and outdoors.

An untidy house among the angels
Who lived in large untidy houses,
You were to end your days in a wild expanse
Among brutes who died among friends
In a tame cage I was brought up in.

And admitting less, loud about all and
Shaking head forever, quiet about all,
Silent about little, to say just that,
Taciturn about the lot, and to affirm the lot,
In constrained circumstances I was to begin my life.

You succumbed in a dirty hut
Saying nothing among brutes who died
Accepting all that came in small neat houses
—And never a garden, with hidden cells
Or public halls, vast with open air.

REQUIREMENTS FOR LIGHTNING

Grip me with the strength a baby
Uses when it grips
The extended thumb of an adult.

Bare your appetite;
Goad me with whispered extremes
And patrols of the hand.

Lamps are shady; if encouraged
By a lack of vision, feelers
In the dark may steep their prongs.

THE CANDLE

The candle perched on the radiant shore
Gobbling what remained of shadow;
Candle with a harpy's claw,
Savagery that ravished the shadow.

Shadow ravaging damaged the candle:
Appetite consumed her wick.
Vital the shade to vivid candle,
Wasted by her fatal trick.

BOYS' DAY FESTIVAL

Realising the tremendous stimulation
Of such titles as "Look to the Future"
And "Shape of Things to Come"
More and more compilers of show schedules
Are including them in competitive
Classes — one of the great delights
Is that it opens new fields to the flower arranger.

"High Summer", a phrase that nowadays
Seems to have little meaning
Should bring the big succulent family
To see how the sheen of metal
Enhances a side-table which is placed
In front of the closed, draped curtain for impact.

MRS DALE

I'm glad Jim decided to move out of town.
Here, above everything, trees are less imposed upon:
As he has plenty of time on his hands
He can busy himself with his precious slides.

I was quite struck by the weather yesterday
—Literally heaps of autumn shadow.
Just to remember we read from the diary,
Quietly, careful of Janet downstairs.

It's bliss having traffic as light as the country
Unlike some neighbourhoods. Recently
I seem to have made some progress with the news
Which as a diarist is my stock-in-trade.

Ever so often one bumps into friendly old
Faces one hasn't seen in ages;
Ridding oneself, in a minute's chat,
Of so many grim or dismal pages.

Has one ever lived, I wonder,
Severed from the daily, on the outskirts of a town or a city,
Or upon the hills above — if there are any?
In the case of this particular

Part of the world there are indeed
—Though not the sort you may get a glimpse of
In some other town or city
Less entrenched in our own sort of scenery.

Where we are, though, Frinton Way
Stretches the length of a rise or incline:
Giving both myself and Jim,
Who's not been himself since he gave up smoking,

Quite a considerable spot of bother
On our way back from wherever we've been
—For the time being we haven't a car:
And this makes rather a climb at our age

Out of what otherwise might have been
An ordinary — if not exacting — stroll
Up from the bus stop thirty yards
Along the much busier road at the bottom.

THERE YOU ARE

So if you must be you you must
If you're the way you're feeling
Not that you can say for sure you never
Met this you of yours the loneliness
Of you all and what have you
Cutting you loose from all yours
Except yourself of course
You the paths you can't imagine
Mellow delight of you discovering
What you meant when you sat with this back
To that your look equivocating
About whose front yours was
Well you might while you were slowly

What are you on about now why ask
The usual how do you do how are you
Ever to say you never can tell
With the likes of you who never saw
Your like yourself you with your face
Like an amphitheatre quite beside yourself
Wherever you sat you might remind
Your you know what that here you went back
On yourself to your earlier you
You and your recital yours throughout
You see your abrupt your mock violence
Like talking through a brick wall

IDLE PROMONTORY

The race hanging up to dry
A close up drifted off:
Upside down to what it should be
Little or nothing doubled up.
The dead end up till now underneath
Ended up open-ended.

Rather than run out of after-effects
Out of its dense wobbling
Down and out alongside
The uppermost spread out a zig-zag
Inside out for those for and against
Laid out at sixes and sevens.

Left over right, right over left!
A half-hitch over the eight
—But Overton is off his block.
Over to you, over and out,
As the after-effects in overalls
Overbalance without a shout.

A REFUSAL

Old wounds mouth their fears.
The very thought
Sends shivers down my spine.
I may not stretch a finger beyond the cave
Without a drenching.

Down in the wretched grove
Beast and Beauty consummate their raptures
And assume each other's part
With militant promiscuity:
Odours pour from an array of apertures.

Solitary cells breed their own kin.
Under close scrutiny
Any inch reveals a mass of germs,
Wriggling millions.

OBSOLESCENT CATHEDRAL

Here held sway the dread, breast-plated
Lord of Hosts, whose tent outvied
The Odeon's dome in gloom and in the boom
Of recitations less immured in piacle.
Girder and vitrine still preserve
Memories of that nebulous age
Blown beyond reach. A last cortège
Traces mercurial ripples to infernal yards.

Departure's shrine, where vast congregations
Ever attended the hour to disperse
Until the platform slid from their dream:
Now they huddle in third class urns
Equipped with sandwiches for the journey.

Swifter and thriftier faiths put out
The puff of monumental censers.
Hastening pilgrims shun this station;
Ruined by neglect, it lacks
The sacred aura of predestination.
Those who depend on the local services
Hallow the place now: humdrum Gods.

Thirsts in the drought of night have urged
Us gibberers here, who may abuse
No votress but a punch-drunk vendor;
Indisposed, though belaboured, to impart
Plump cartons of oracular milk.

INSIDE THE PALACE

Deep in these timeless stretches breathed a pause
where the deranged dogroses sheathed their claws;
      when he arrived there, his hair in dishevel,
he might well have thrown off the covers of sleep
      (beneath which the dairymaid tickles the Devil)
everything stood intact — at a leap.
      But in disrepair. After years of neglect
    rhododendrons tunnelled down the once correct
    avenues, where in the old days
dandies, in their baroque comportments,
      plucked attentive sprays.
Wisteria dangled its imperial livery from the state apartments.
    With a faraway look in its grey eyes,
    a stone hermaphrodite loitered, wise
as Minerva, in a court; all that was living dozed.
      Cow parsley drowsed pungently where it had
           [with insolence
sought audience with the sleeping throne. Closed
      were the royal shutters. Viscount Somnolence
    was regent here. And grey from lack of light,
    mirrored halls were bereft of sight;
not even the intruder's shape could penetrate
      their icy surface. As was fated,
reaching the chamber where she lay in state,
      he lost his nerve. The doorknob hesitated.

"Why am I here? The dream awake inside her
is bemused by a sunrise perpetually fanning wider.
          Unblemished, the hangings of dimity lace,
the crisp white layers,
               vacantly framing the crisp white face
which moves its lips as if in silent prayer.
          What does she await? My kiss or her favourite pony's?
          She may be more agile than ever a daughter of
                                        [Schœney's,
               but over his mane she drapes her glimmering hair.
Am I to suffer some translation
               at the bedside? Oh, I dare
say she would nuzzle me between inhalation and exhalation,
               and then remember her manners.
          Out comes the trousseau, the family banners:
regrettable etiquettes, æons behind the times.
               The necessary mansions of our restored selves
are in contrary, incompatible climes;
               I'm full of dragons, she's all pixies and elves.
          Something avoids me in this palace,
               yet it annuls my quest — Alas!
This chamber, pervaded by the breath
               of a sleeping wood; my eyes are sore
from lack of the same commodity, tears or death.
               From her four-poster vibrates an occasional
                                        [snore."

Outdoors, night crouched close to the ground.
Low over the wood, the moon looked round:
a nude grown numb in her pose.
Warthogs chuckled in the midgy brakes;
dark trees oozed their gums. Dew froze
on the grass-blades. Softer than a snake's
hiss, a wind sung through the sacred groves
in the distance, covering giants' graves.
There were no forthcoming attractions;
the day's adventure had been stowed away
in some obscure pigeon-hole, among distractions
such as Chinese puzzles, *thés*
dansants, odd crystal slippers, his gloves:
another unpaid entry, under "Soiled Doves".
His Highness longed for familiar comforts: pages.
But now it was late. Hacking his homeward path,
he might find himself nowhere — for ages.
Within the ruin tinkled a girlish laugh.
". . .And the jealous dogrose, I eluded her snare,
now even the dogrose does not care.
Why should a dogrose care?
Sunk in the enjoyment of her own odour,
dans un palais de rose pure."
Thus was he waylaid on the verandah.

And all that was living. . .loitered. Faraway
from the courts, from the state apartments. . .Grey
eyes of the hermaphrodite. . .
And the witch of the place grew sleepy. Laughter
in the timeless stretches. . .Night. . .
ever after. . .

AN ANGRY BLUE

How to be reason, how to be hopeless in light:
Exhaustion throwing off the bad
Other proposals — letter to get off
To people of pedestrian letters, petitions

Somebody causes out of gas bills, *idées fixes.*
Falling and tardiness in keeping up
Dental Floss, feet. Highly strung times
To sit still through for long enough, guilt about

Times unstrung when one can't get up
In the shambles that has somehow ended up.
Of a kitchen of the body — blisters, bruises,
Spots brought on by not changing to be

Bright for all efforts to prove oneself
A citizen: that has been denied fellow citizens.
Without blame. Imagination, a dirty enough
Word, an education, it elbows. And walls

Of the innumerable discomforts brought about.
But sleepiness, the fading eyes, the heavy.
Heavy to waste an hour, the mending
Of petty ruptures, all the tasks—

How to be hated, having no whine
Among children, throwing off the dream.
And power trips, and self obliterating ideas
And scent of recriminations. Yet another

Pedestrian in charge makes jams.
Being so over-sensitive, falling back asleep,
Guilt about sanitary habits such as
The person who wishes you dead

When one doesn't manage to do anything
Out of the chair facing the cooker
In the hotch-potch of aches in the corners
And irritating underwear. Often enough

To be clean and unblemished as a new advertisement,
That has been denied a citizen:
Other than imagining not having had enough
Of when one feels too old to do anything

About heads held upright by anyone,
By being what we are, especially heartedness
Of an infinity done over, sleep,
The semi-faint and shock blanking out.

A further, deeper breath of lapsing
Into oblivion. How to be swayed by
Swaying eyes disunited, blanking out to sleep
And sleep a second time again.

YOUR BODY IS ALL

Your body is all angles and balances
Like my mind. The shape of you
Is silence where things are posed.
Such things as are heard of,
Imagined, but never seen, I touch
When I hold you inexpertly
Before you go in from the rain.
Then I am left with a maidenly rain
Inside me, and cannot tell
Which way is home.

DOWN UNDER

After two days, civilisation is either above us
    or below us.
Here, where the stone bird plummets out of the tree,
    where random fauna exists
    by virtue of its linguistic possibility,
    I can still smell you apart
    from the grass trees, tree ferns and fern birds.
Should the Gargantuan shoulder-blades shudder or twitch,
    all the pink wrigglies will tumble back
    into the oceans, and the Acacia,
    with its own peculiar stratum of combinations
    in the layer cake of the cultures,
    will join its weeping forces to recolonise
    their citadels' marzipan memorials.
Below the sandstone precipice, deep in ravines,
    among charred trees as lonely, as enchanted
    as maidenhair, or any cedern chasm;
    athwart Bluegums, the trippers thread a tiny sequence
    of ant incidents — only their gestures fibrillate
    in thickets screening them from the distance in ks;
    their hemispheres beneath hat-rims.
The stereophonic sonar collisions
    manage to not quite superimpose or eclipse each other
    with a studied nonchalance whose virtuosity
    is to sound accidental.
Should this Atlas shrug. . .
Dimity overhead, a fern of rain sweeps across.
The tiny silver Transport Fish,
    quitting the shoal spiralling above the State of Excitement,
    heads off, above the bight, above cirrus,
    into the empyrean, towards the Holy City
    —its glint diminishing over the Nullarbor.

Sufficiency Knob and Patience Well: between Point Moody
    and Lake Disappointment there are no cities.
And on the continent of the suburbs, the girl from Marble Bar
    jogs daintily over the bush adders:
    these are to be ground to powder
    in order to fertilise our ubiquitous bungalow jungles
    among the Banksias.
Hard graft and slick, and stretches of bird assist
    the wedding of the Wattle with Poinsettia.
Since when, each family has a right to their back gardens,
    to their own roof over their heads,
    above banana: corrugated Nissen gullies
    —junctions where they can harvest the bees.

PAVING STONES

Dim crags teach your giddy namesakes
Lack of fright, kids, learn from pavements.
Yours is a steeper path than theirs:
Be agile, tempt unwary cars.
Only teatime threatens. Hold it.
Drag feet, whine, and baulk retirement.
Worst of exasperating neighbours.
Next day ruins every plot:
Entombed in suits, you reappear
Smarter than Hell Himself, grown up.
Flourish your chalks, the pavement stretches
Blemished arms for you to adorn.
Batter cans. A brave sun coughs his last.
Worry the handcuffs shut by the hush
Whose proper name politeness asks indoors:
When raving Silence stares
Lips are forbidden to gesticulate.

Earliest dark is yours. Stay hid.
Play late beneath the sky's suggestive blanket.
Make of sensuous rules a game
Or drown — the rising night of Man
Floods, overflows, your areas, attics.
Damage done by prowling streets
Can't be anaemic. Scream out. Bleed.
Or cease to feel your tragedies.
Civil, the stones beneath your feet,
And parched for darkest blood, fresh spilt.
In every way you walk on these.

EXTRACT FROM AN ESSAY ON LOVE

Don Juan's not the man who makes love to women,
But one to whom women make love.
He holds onto his reason for as long as he can.
Don José in a rage, emphasising his uncontrollable temper,
Once, verging on madness,
Killed someone who cheated him in a card game.
Don't! secretes secrets.
"Free was I born, and free will I die."
And to die triumphantly outside the *corrida*
Seems to be universal. They die as deeply in love,
To wander in the wild outlaw-infested Spanish mountains.

THE QUESTION

A hardy perennial — is it to leave no trace
    like fish through the water or birds through the air?
Often we become clad in its aura
    when least conscious of what we are wearing
    —deep in the letter from the Far West,
    while the sunset spills through panes.
    reaching our blue dress and the blue chair.
While it might well be lift-off, it is never the in-flight movie;
    though its anathema, ugliness, may be no easier to exemplify
    —chicken innards on the bitumen outside the restaurant
    kitchen door; carparks it will be difficult
    to find a use for, after the demise of cars;
    or offices where automated decisions
    are fodder for shredders — the waste of trees.
But out beyond progress, that host of Phoenixes, the bush
    burning and renewing itself partakes of the order
    we associate with this; and it is fitting
    not to interfere but to bury one's debris and the remnants,
    to unpile any stones one has piled together,
    and to fill up the holes one has scooped in the sand.

Perhaps it's a train called Ken,
    flowers in a vase on the doily in a saucer
    on the table on the carpet
    covering the parquet in the alcove.
To form chains or to break habits.
Anything you say it may use in evidence against you;
    establishing the laws of its being
    only that these may be broken — like a mirror
    whose reflections are invented.
It is five objects, rather than fifteen.

However, whilst admitting that it is to be imperceptible
in the landscape, to vanish into it
rather than to stand out against it,
there is also the ravishment of a child's pathetic
clockwork machine turned umber by exposure
—rust, and the becoming of a relic.
Brash silveriness and the shining fantasias of the Cadillac.
The details, the myriad man-made things:
the winder, the head-frame, the skip;
saucepan and thermos; the bellows,
the wheelbarrow and the churn.
As much in the learning of names
as in the appraisal of their entities—
appreciation of the jack-hammer, the spoon-tool,
and the Beehive sock-knitting machine.
Broken jalopies, like beetles unable to right themselves;
monuments to the inaccessibility of their differentials.
Something to be stumbled upon
rather than turned craftily on the approved wheel.
Its trunk pushes upwards through the oil-drum.
A sensation of surprise recognised.
The gap of light between buttocks and thighs
—or darkness — it is the well.

BABEL

The electric sun and the looking moon,
This great indoors — a secret grew with the rain
Until his tower of eloquence reached the roof.
But if a toy grow tall as light
A lasting curse will add its grown-up name:
Some thunderclap whose patronym
Is dark for hauteur forks our tongue
(The prince's fear of swapping with the bullfrog),
Shadow operates our gloves,
And on the night a veil solidifies.

But each beclouded word remains opaque
Only as long as the dawn takes to filter through hessian;
Then shall a wealth of birds applaud the proscenium,
And a plush crocodile interrogate the children
While you hide behind a palm:
Heads that are staked on each finger
Crane over the edge to peer at the audience
Though the theatre stand empty as a deserted telephone booth—
Because a thing so tricky to put up
Could never be that easily dismantled.

Acknowledgements

'Notions of a Mirror' appeared in the *P.E.N. Poetry Anthology 1971-72;* 'Deficiencies of Tourism', 'Examining Mine, Imagining Yours' and 'Myth among Boulders' all appeared in *The Scotsman;* 'Animal Lover' appeared in *Antaeus.* 'Femina Deserta' was first published as a pamphlet by Softly Loudly Books. 'Mrs Dale' was first published in a pamphlet of new poems for the Poetry Book Society in 1973. 'Modern Sonnets' appeared in *Wallpaper Magazine,* and 'Dreamt Lives' in *Vanessa Magazine.* 'Babel' was first published in *Vogue.* 'Inside the Palace' appeared in *Poetry Review,* as did 'Drought'.